# Branches

## Maurice Thomas

Charleston: Createspace
the Amazon Group

## ACKNOWLEDGMENTS—

The author is grateful to editors who selected the following poems for their publications: "Measuring Water Oaks," "Crazy Old Lilly," "Wild Yellow Plums," "Snake Handler at the Fair," "Late-Summer Cricket," "Bone Memories," and "Flowering Bloodroot" first appeared in *Doors*, an anthology of seven poets from Red Dust Books, New York. *Cold Mountain Review* published "Season of the Dark Green Leaf," and *Tar River Poetry* published "White Oak." "Jennie Copeland" and "April" appeared in *Wind*. "The Crossing" was published by *Kakalak*. Several poems were published in the Huntsville Literary Society's *Poem* including "The Garner House," "Pond Spirit," "Side Trip," "Above Fredericksburg," and others. "Great Wagon Road Home" received the Hayman America Award from the NC Poetry Society. The author also contributed to Wingate University's *Counterpoint* which he and fellow English Department colleague Sylvia Little-Sweat edited for many years.

ISBN 13:978-1478322221
ISBN: 10:1478322225

Copies of the book are available in the Wingate University Bookstore, Wingate, NC 28174, Createspace estore at Createspace.com, and Amazon.com. Signed copies are also available from the author at PO Box 313, Wingate, NC 28174. $20 includes shipping and handling.

*for*
*my wife*
Pamela
*and*
*daughter*
Lauren
*who share*
*my love for*
*all things*
*English,*
*Scottish,*
*Irish,*
*Welch*

# Contents

# Harmony

We come from the hills of the Blue Ridge
searching for our ancient Celtic home
by old hedgerows and stacked rock walls
marking these Isles in green and grey.
The marrow of our bones is webbed
Anglo-Saxon, Norman, Scot, Irish, Welch.
We are from your scattered seed that
rooted out the rock of the New World.
Our song is hypnotic harmony and drone
filled with old longing and lament,
fixed in pipes, strung on fiddle and bow
to set us reeling in a whiskey clog or jig.
We feel the weight of stone, the yoke,
the hunger groan, your stubborn will.
We know the ancient sounds we hear-
*dun, dale, burn, tun, ton, glen, ash, lin.*
We stand on cliffs high above the sea
to feel the restless Atlantic breathe
honeysuckle breath that lured all west.

One clap-
a thousand gull wings
open like a white fan
over Galway Bay.

# Sunday Morning in St Patrick's, Dublin

*for Colin*

This place was Latin Catholic first with Celtic tongue
before Henry named it Anglican for the English Pale.
I had come to find the tomb of Jonathan Swift
and see the ironic window that Guinness left but
surrendered instead to the spell of the Eucharist sung:
*Agnus Dei, qui tollis pecata mundi, miserere nobis.*
*Agnus Dei, qui tollis pecata mundi, dona nobis pacem.*
It was not the word nor wafer dipped in wine but that
organ toccata of shattered crystals falling through sun
when religion fell away, only faith remained that I felt
communion with the living but longing for the dead.
*Beatae memoriae Deo gratias.*

## Cliffs of Moher

We are here for an hour
by limestone cliffs formed
in the bed of a tropical sea
350 million BC.

# The Burren

Ireland's ancient Celtic face
of cracked limestone,
hills of flat clints
like tombstones carved
by the Gulf's wind and rain,
softened by tufts of crane's bill
and yellow bird's foot trefoil-
a place for wings and burrow
but not man-
last refuge of the Celts
with their backs to the cliffs:
'Not water enough
to drown a man,
not tree enough
to hang a man,
nor soil enough
to bury a man,'
place of will-o-the-wisp mist,
fairy whispers in white thorn
where at sunset, it's said,
people of the Sidhe
slip from the Otherworld
through cairns and mounds
to roam the portal tombs,
tangle our hair and toss
our troubled dreams.

**1922**

Time and rage unlocked
the ornate Georgian door
and ripped it frame and all
from the Irish Shore.

## Bone Memories

The end should come
without beginning-
sudden hurt that sears,
not the long panic,
reshuffled dread,
not the rotting love.
Come quickly
bone and memories-
only these are
white washed clean.

There is a grotto
deep in woods
beyond the castle wall
where, if you go there,
the only escape
is dreaming.

Spiked beaks betray
the lichen knot a nest
of young hummingbirds
riding a windy limb.
Their new eyes
are startled by sun
on down and petal.
Yet when the beak and
crimped wings are ready,
they do not resist
the pull of feathers
but spill easily
from nest
toward nectar.

# By this narrow crossing of the world

they left their names in chalk on the white cliffs—
the invaders--Germanic Angles, Saxon, Jutes who
pushed the Celts into the fringe of Arthurian mist
when Latin Britannia the legions of Caesar left.
In time Danes laid claim and bartered with Alfred
till death came and Cnut's brief Viking reign.
The last of the Saxons Edward the Confessor
left vacant the throne of England for William
the Norman who signed his name in Anglo-French
and relegated Saxon survivors with their old English
to the final judgment of the Doomsday Book.
Celtic, Latin, Saxon, Angles, Danish, Norman-
all woven into the knotted English tapestry,
their marks now are faded streaks of black flint
on the white face of Britain no invader has carved
for these thousand years, not Spanish Armada
nor Hitler's *Luftwaffe* downed by hurling Spitfires
diving like angry, black tipped fulmars guarding
their home nests high on the cliffs above Dover.

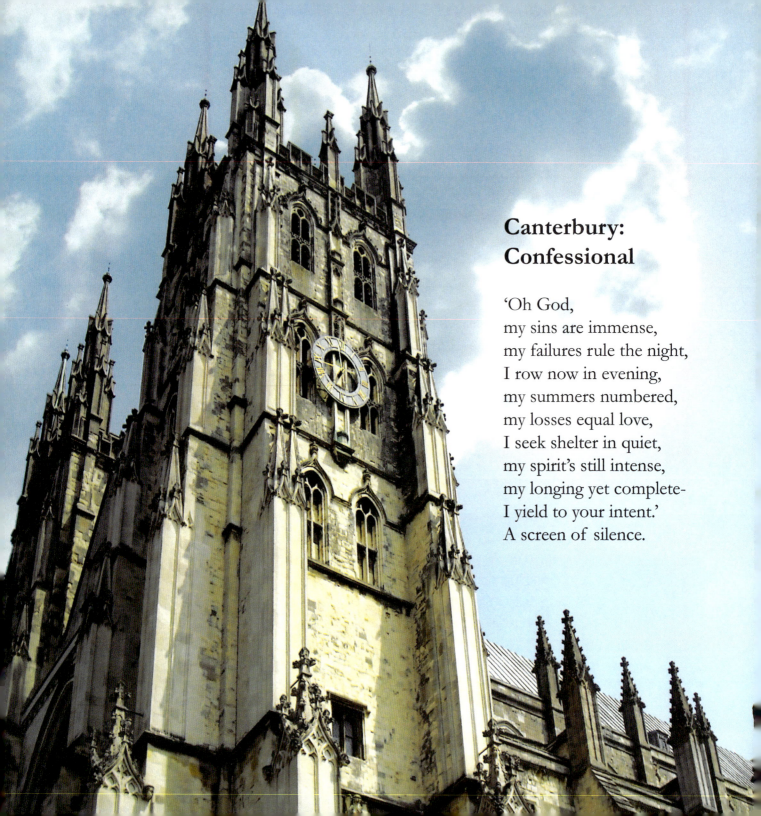

## Canterbury: Confessional

'Oh God,
my sins are immense,
my failures rule the night,
I row now in evening,
my summers numbered,
my losses equal love,
I seek shelter in quiet,
my spirit's still intense,
my longing yet complete-
I yield to your intent.'
A screen of silence.

In diamond reign
we wait her arrival
on the royal balcony
where on time
she waves to us
and we wave back,
completing the need
for fantasy.

## Remembrance Day in London

I watch the English lay
blood red poppies with
black dead eyes on
the marble steps
of the Cenotaph then
silence—only
the rattling of ragged
sycamore leaves.
I have heard before
this rasping sigh,
'Remember me'
and held the ache
of falling leaves
from white sycamores.
Do we march to remember
or be remembered
in this long journey
from fire to stone to flower
to flesh and finally love?
Our shuffling feet
among crushed leaves
and muffled cry beg,
'Remember me.'
We march because
we know at end all
are red paper poppies
on white marble
the wind will tear away.
Our only hope is stone,
a Cenotaph, where touch
the living and dead—
the spark is memory.

When your're weary and weaned of the world may clouds
of hydrangea chart the way through evening's light.

   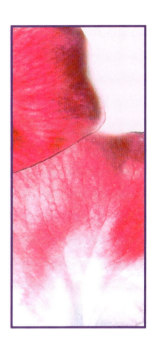

## Ceremony

What fire has left, let wind lift with rose petals of home
and scatter over stones first touched by morning sun
and last, kindled light when day is done,
these ashes of one we loved.

# Sung Eucharist

Morning in Westminster
we wait the Procession,
watch the September sun,
shouldered by twelve apostles,
climb the great rose window
in small steps of blue and green and gold,
then stain wine red the white communion.
In this place with Gothic pillars of bone
where music is balanced in stone,
we sit blinded in shafts of cracked light
that ancestors bent through glass.
All wait in need of Penitence and Absolution.
In every temple shrine, mosque, and dome
we bask in chosen light, receive our Intercession,
prisoners of a prism where the whole is lost in holy.
We are violet, they are blue; some choose scarlet,
others yellow from the varied, divided hue.
What is true? The sun moves beyond our will.
We spread our prayer rugs, unroll old scrolls,
light our incense, break the wafer, strike a bell,
and drink each other's blood while silent
stars move to geneses beyond our meager hills.
*Sanctus, Benedictus: dona nobis pacem.*

*Westminster Abbey*
*London 9/ll/03*

Only ten stand in mute stone above
Westminster's Great West Door too narrow
for more of the 20th Century's Christian martyrs-
First is Friar Kolbe who volunteered a death at Auschwitz
beside South Africa's Mazemola baptized in converted blood,
then Luwun who stood alone against Ugandan madness
next to Russia's Grand Duchess Elizabeth, sister to the poor,

whose hymns still ring in the darkness of Bolshevik's pits.
In the middle is America's preacher King, shielding a child,
with Salvador's saint Romero who died lifting a defiant Cup.
To the right is uniter Bonheoffer hanged by Germany's *verfuhrer*
and the murdered Qamar Zia who left Islam to become Esther John,
finally the Papuan teacher Tapiede killed by invaders of New Guinea
with Miao Christian Zhiming who would not bow to Mao's Revolution-
faces of the faceless dead whose words still wound an impenitent world.

# Earth's Tips Are Burning

Walking from the empty woods,
she saw the two dead hawks
hanging from the bare sycamore tree,
the dry jeweled eyes staring
through broken wings.
For three days she had watched them
high above the creek
with morning in their feathers.
They had circled his contempt
until he blew them out of the sky.
She knew.
He killed everything.
What he could not reach
he cursed or shot.
She was all she had left.
Their screaming children had run away
far beyond any neighbor's house.
This night he would wake again in sweat,
feeling the blood vessels they had
pulled like earth worms from his legs
crawling around his heart.
She waited in the shadow of the moon
until he stirred and saw perched on bed posts
the two hawks with flared wings
and felt the sudden beaks
tear the vessels out even
before he could scream.
She lifted the hawks and placed them on the coals,
watching them pop and singe in smoke and flight.
Tomorrow she would sell his guns,
buy herself a dress and hope for spring.
She was sure she was through with men.

Tall St Martin-in-the-Fields anchors the corner of rowdy Trafalgar.

# Waiting by an Empty Porch

The old gods are beggars now
in the shadows of St Paul's
where Enlil rustles leaves with a sigh
in the dazed eyes of Tonatiuh and Ra.
Spring comes yet Osiris sleeps while
Eostre mends a cast off Easter dress.
Woden, Thor merely mark daily grind,
their thunderbolts lost in lore
for War now wears another face
as do all the children of Zeus.
Where are the augurs now
to interpret the fleeing birds,
the oracles to read Apollo's will?
And when the Eucharist is no more
and all that's left are these empty steps,
what will man be, what will he see
standing on the ruins here or Jerusalem
gazing longingly at the Pleiades?

The clipper *Cutty Sark* grounded now at Greenwich, monument to the British Century.

**'REMEMBER
WINSTON
CHURCHILL'**
emblazoned
on the stone floor
at Westminster's
front door.
STEP LEFT.

Open the door.
It's ten till one.
The Queen
from Buckingham
to Parliament
comes.

45

There was a time
when a poet's weaponry
was carried on the back
of a charging steed
or pierced the intricacies
of courtly love.
Now it's used mostly
to desconstruct what's not.

The kings are dead now,
their terror under glass,
coffers emptied,
divinity spent,
their armor,
a delicate fan,
arranged on castle walls
by red exit signs.
The masses
have taken the hill.

# Poppies at Whitsand

Here where the sea
has stripped Cornwall
to black rock ribs
uprooted in fields,
a bloated autumn sun
fills with gulls crying
like women in burqas.
All night poppies fell.
England remembered
November with petals
dusting blue silence.
Even here no waves
can drown her sorrow:
'On the surface
I'm just like you,
but in my heart
there's a stone,'
Belsen's voice in
Bedlam's museum
'not appropriate for children.'
At Whitsand she comes
dragging her cart
of rags and shoes.
There is no passage here
through bone nor bracken.
We are trapped again
in man's failures.
That new century door
we thought opened
just south of Pagasus
opened on Baghdad.

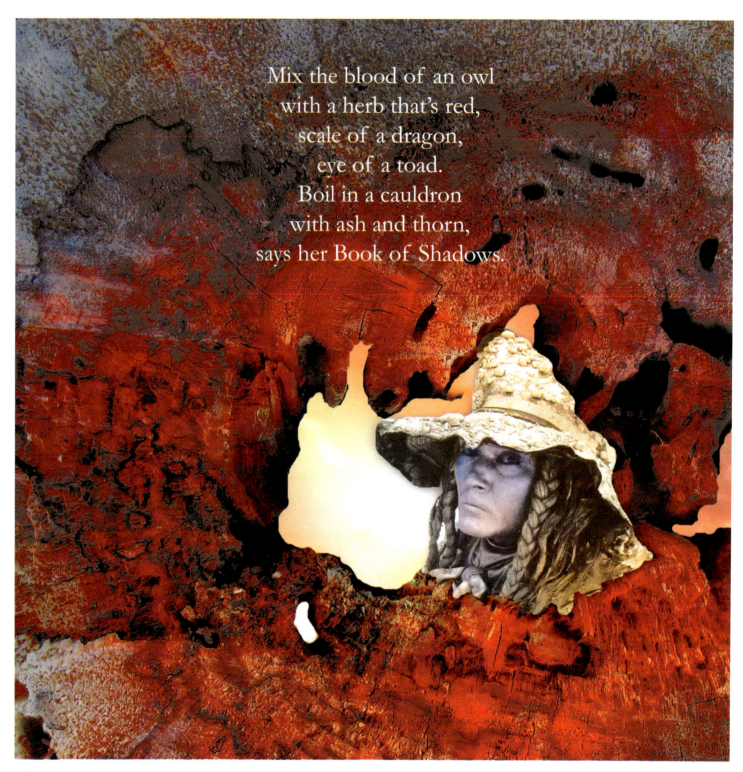

Mix the blood of an owl
with a herb that's red,
scale of a dragon,
eye of a toad.
Boil in a cauldron
with ash and thorn,
says her Book of Shadows.

Come sip, my dear, this red chokeberry wine.

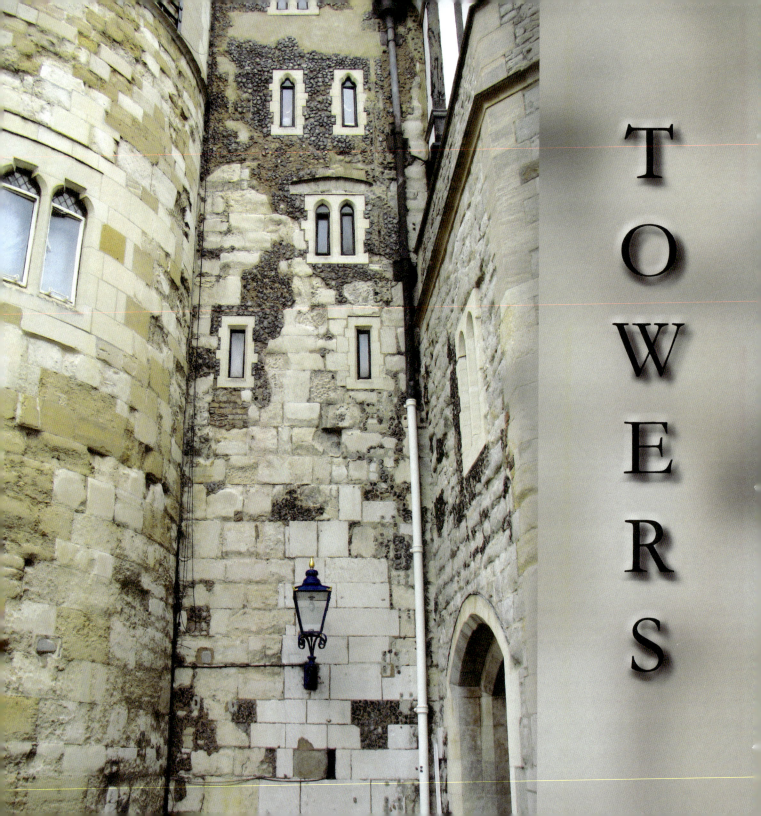

TOWERS

When God came down at Shinar
confounding the babbling builders,
the tribes in their scattered heads carried away
the bogus prints for the stepping stones to Heaven.
'Ra Ra Ra,' they shouted from the top of Giza
to the Trojans carrying their stones to Illium.
Then in the dark time of the great cathedrals
they sharpened their walls into spires of divinity
often in competition with vaulting rivals though
most built to spot their enemies, keep unruly wives,
or let a lout earn knighthood by climbing a wall,
dangling on the golden braid of Rapunzel.
Eiffel steel freed the builders from stone's reality.
Now even the minarets of Mecca are dwarfed
by the soaring Makkah with its clock marking Haj
and rival Burj Khalifa above the oil wells of Dubai.
On the top floors of Petronas One in Kuala Lumpur,
men refine their algorithms and mingle like gods,
far beyond the reach of a Lancelot or even Roland
where not Rapunzel but the witch is waiting.

London's new Canary Wharf on the Isle of Dogs climbs the Queen's Tulip Stairs at old Greenwich.

At Trafalgar
the four lions
molded from the
melted cannons
of Waterloo
stare back
black as Napoleon's
flattened
three cornered hat.

## Thames Crossing

Of the bridges over the Thames the Tower
in blue is most showy though Westminster,
green as the seats in the House of Commons,
was the inspiration for Wordsworth the poet.
The Lambeth wears its royal red situated
near the House of Lords and Blackfriars
next to Waterloo by Hungerford spans both
tide and time from the old Templars' church
to the power station that's now Tate Modern.
But London Bridge is far more famous for
'falling down, falling down' to stop the Danes
from overtaking King AEthelred the Unready,
then rebuilt in 1209 by Henry II as penance for
the murder of one-time friend Thomas Becket,
who placed the martyr's chapel in the center
by the stacked houses, shops, public latrines.
It soon became a fire trap tunnel ending at
the black servered head of William Wallace.
In Tudor times the wives of Henry VIII
passed the sagging grins of courtly lovers,
traveling to a final date through Traitors' Gate.
Three hundred tarred heads once hung in a row
not counting Thomas More and Walter Raleigh
or the disinterred scowl of Cromwell the Puritan.
After 600 years the old bridge gave way to
early 19th century modern, the one the Brits
sold to the American so that tourists might cross
a phantom Thames at Lake Havasu, Arizona.

# Cherokee Canoe

Leave your cell phone, lose yourself,
wade with me into the New River where
ancestors crossed from Virginia in 1790's.
With saw, maul, and wedge they split
the wilderness into homes on the Blue Ridge
among doomed chestnut and Cherokee.
Lift the canoe till we find deep water.
Row with me beneath the canopy of hemlock,
yellow birch and wind-combed willow.
Feel with your oars the river's pebble bed,
fragments of gneiss from Appalachia's heart.
These ancient rocks were their stepping stones,
these waters the silver fingers pointing the way.
In the basement of your brains is the trunk
buckled by leather straps holding hope and daring,
carried over the Atlantic from Blandford in Britain,
hauled through the mountains to here and now.
This river, these hills with mist of blue bird-foot violet,
hickory and hobblebush, of buckeye and bittersweet,
these mountains where the Great Buzzard of the Cherokee
dipped a dark wing in the soft earth and pushed up,
they are yours to salvage from new assaults.
Float now for there's no going back.
Run with the river that knows the way to the balance
of water, chestnut, hollow, hill, and man.
See the bridge ahead? It is the bridge to everywhere
or nowhere at all. You choose, but first open the trunk.

from an 1830 etching of Blandford Forum, County Dorcet, England

# John Osborne, Diarist, et al

Great-grandfather's grandfather John--
not the John buried beneath the floor
of St. Peter St. Paul in Blandford whose father
Robert owned the Greyhound tavern and inn
and whose great-great grandson George
crossed the New River in the1790's--
kept a diary in the Waxhaws from 1800 to '21
of drought, pulling down corn, courting, drinking,
tramping wheat, boils, mumps, Methodist camp meetings,
horseback trips to Charlotte, Camden, Charleston
and who made his money for land distilling corn whiskey
then died in 1861, two years before his grandson
was so terrorized by the smoke and fire and death
during Picket's Charge that he swore to God he'd
became a devout member of Smyrna Methodist
Episcopal Church-South if he ever got home to farm
the land his grandfather bought on Lanes Creek near
where your great-grandfather, the direct descendent
of Rev. Tristram who served in 1558 as rector
for St. Nicholas Church in Surry, England
-no relation to the John who lived in Dorset-
cleared the bottom land with a horse and dynamite
and was the only son of your great-great grandfather
who died at Fredericksburg on the same hill
as your other great-great grandfather's brother

who never made it to Gettysburg but was thinking of his
uncle's dream to push a wheelbarrow around the world
never to know he got as far as Lancaster, South Carolina,
but came back with two watermelons & three cantaloupes
but was later found hanging by the neck in the barn
the Yankees burned on their way up from Atlanta
according to your great-grandfather who found his
own blue-eyed bastard son in a basket at the church door
the morning they went to bury his mother who had
remarried a Collins and lost all the land of the man
who went off to Fredericksburg and never returned to
see his grandson-- not your grandfather who loved baseball
and married the part German woman from Oklahoma
who was questioned by the FBI for her speeches in WWII
whose father-in-law loved corn whiskey so much
he left his wife and son to open a tavern that
burned down twice along with half the town--
I'm referring to your other grandfather who could
square a house with a string but lived so long
he forgot his name whose son learned of the diary
from his 99 year old spinster aunt and church organist
who kept everything in a trunk that connected it all
which you may not be able to keep straight
but is there right now tangled in your DNA,
singed by fire and corn whiskey, but there's
really no cause to worry nor be concerned
since you took after your grandmother,
but let's not get into all that!

## White Oak

I come here mostly
for the way winter oaks
shape this house and hill
and cold sap moves hidden
in darkness through hard wood.
There was never much warmth here,
only strength of having endured
all things save love.
If I told you
I know a woman
whose soft wet lips
turn me to fire,
would you break once
even into laughter?

All Westminster in the blink of the London Eye.

# Golden Altar of Morning

We'll step away from the cliff,
find a path to the river's edge,
strip bare and wade in to wash
the oil and acid stain from skin,
stand at the golden altar of morning
to make our offering-
a river rock, bough of maple leaf
bound with all our dreams
and wait for the river to speak
the language of the spirit world:
*What was will not come again*
*lest we die.*
But what will come again?
*The chestnut tree will come again*
*when west and east form one.*
*The raccoons will come again*
*to feed from open hands.*
*The Cherokee will sing again.*
*The oaks will climb to crown*
*bald tips of earth again*
*and the rivers of the world*
*will run clean and clear again.*
*You will not die again.*

## 139 to Waterloo

London-the name, heavy as lions,
not prissy Paris, but solid English oak,
beef Wellington, hard green peas,
taste of stone, bitter black ale.
Wash from us all that's America
and you'll find English hearts
filled with primal longing.
Oh let us ride your tall red bus
down Baker's Street past Portman Square,
turn at Selfridge's pricey corner
and squeeze up Oxford by Bond,
take a left on Regent, dodge Eros' arrow
and the wet hooves of Haymarket,

then pass eyeball to eyeball the
black lions of Trafalgar crouching
in the shadow of St Martin-in-the Fields,
turn down the broad Strand
tipping our caps to the Savoy,
circling Aldwych to Somerset House,
pausing on Waterloo Bridge to snap
a golden Parliament, a pale St Paul's
anchored by the shimmering Thames,
arriving just in time at the station
to hop the caged Jubilee Line
all the way home to St John's Wood
where we will rise in steps of light and
rest at last in the garden of the Queen.

Come spring
we will weave
boughs of cedar,
dress in fern
and speak
in the tongue
of frog and bird
until the queen
of the meadow
crowns summer.

# Great Wagon Road Home

With their lives in their pockets
James's Scotch-Irish left
the wound of Ireland to square
a dream in backwoods America.
Land-legs in Pennsylvania, ox cart loaded,
taste of honeysuckle wilderness on lips,
down the Great Wagon Road they came
across the Schuylkill at crowded Philadelphia
through Lancaster and Harris Ferry on Sesquehanna
on to the Potomac and across the valley of Virginia,
joining German, Irish, and English dreamers
pushing through Staunton Gap on the Blue Ridge
and into the frontier of Carolina following
hunting trails of Cherokee and Catawba
to find home under chestnuts by fertile creeks
of the New, the Broad, Yadkin, Tuckasegee.
They notched and squared huts in clearings,
burned the land for corn and garden,
love and dreamed deep in corn shuck mattresses,
filled cabins with children, their eyes blue chicory,
drank persimmon beer and sassafras tea,
grew strong on hominy, pork and honey.
They believed in a farmer's God,
the strength of a man's arm,
talked of freedon, fought Cornwallis,
built the oak cradle of Jackson's democracy.

# Side Trip

*for Tress Stanifer*

What to do with Aunt Tress from Oklahoma
who laughs at 75 and has seen New Zealand.
All we have after a family slideshow is
upper South Carolina unstained by royal
tidewater history or azalea—mere sand hills
of jack pines, turkey houses, and watermelons.
By Friday, talked out and needing adventure,
we drive the back roads looking for 40 Acre Rock,
a local wonder of bald, pine scratched granite.
There is no way to make it Morocco or Glacier Bay,
just a forty acre rock stuck in steamy South Carolina.
On the way out we find the tree of ripe plums,
its fruit of red and yellow marbles spilt on sand.
The taste is old as childhood, wildly familiar.
We watch as she quietly wraps a wet seed in tissue
to carry home for planting in Oklahoma.

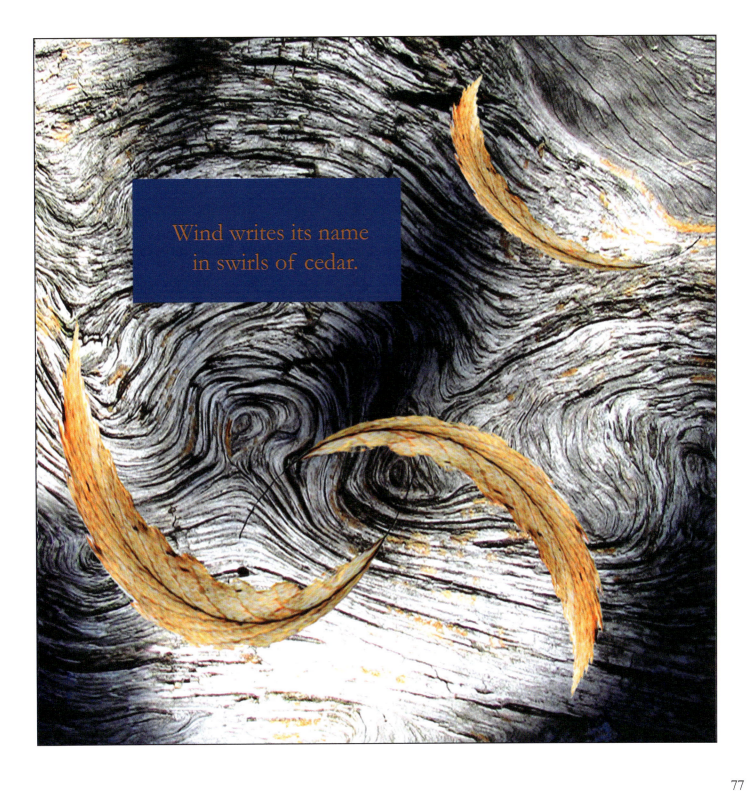

Wind writes its name
in swirls of cedar.

## Wild, Yellow Plums

A tangled patch of wild plums
scorch and pop in a flaming heap
no longer threat to fields
he had watched over half a century.
Always he planned to turn it under
but for the way she went each spring
to find what wild taste would preserve.
Why keep a nuisance now for birds?
The disk harrow turns warm ash to dirt.
It is done. Nephews will have it clean.
He crosses the fields to the empty house.
Behind his back the yellow patch
flies away in a blue jay's beak.

## To find your way

follow the waters
of the creek
to the New River
that will carry you
from the mountains
into the Ohio and
down the Mississippi
to the Gulf
whose warm stream
flows toward home
where waves break
into mist and myth
against the dark stone
of Britain.

# Above Fredericksburg

*For Osborne Thomas*
*d. Dec. 13, 1862*

On Marye's Height
spikes of blazing star
mark the hopeless line
by the stone wall
they held and held
against Burnside's will.
Beside the steepled town
flows the Rappahannock
where death crossed
plank by plank the ice
and frozen fog toward
a red December sun.
You whose image
none living recall,
only a name
and dying words
passed on,
where are the bones?
If I knew the spot,
I would break
your stalk
of purple valor
to carry home.

# Blackberries

Through thorn, wasp,
chigger, and chafed leaf
grow the darkest berries
I watch you pick
one by one staining
fingers, lips, bucket blue.
We've come so far
to taste the earth and
mesh with wonder what
the woods hold secure.
In winter's dread
we'll eat our fill
and mate with summer.

# New River

Here
before the mountains
were lifted,
unknown, unnamed
until we came
trekking the Blue Ridge.
Raptor, mammal, man-
but rippled shadows
on the freckled trout
above your pebble bed.
And who will name you
when we are gone
or hear your song
with stone?

## The Crossing

Standing at the edge of darkness
tempted by light,
the raccoons took the chance,
crossed the boundary
to the glinting tin cup offering—
dry creek taste kernels
of crayfish, egg of wren, dust of bone.
Each night the silver cup filled,
each night a less timorous crossing.
Then—in a quaver of reason,
they lifted the cup in paw hands tipped
with claw and crept into the teeth of darkness.
There on a rock above the creek they waited,
watched moonlight white as manna come
streaming through trees striking the cup silver.
But nothing.
For a week they came even in trembling rain,
watching, waiting.
But nothing.
So—back into the dark,
into the cold certainty of creek things
they moved,
untamed by light
or love
or grace.

## Tuesday-

the need to see, taste, and touch
a thousand years in ten days,
to catch a coughing bus,
wade High Street Kensington,
climb the hungry steps of St Paul's,
choose a moment with Monet
or roam the halls of the V&A.
Done in at Lancaster Gate
we cross to find swans alone
on the still Long Water
all day waiting.

Long I stood
on the shore of grief
holding you in images
the way I held you as child
till I could rule the cold
currents of sorrow,
wade in to the river
by the willows
and  let go.

For a year and a day I've kept the wolves at bay waiting
their turn to the river to stay or time and love to ta⌐

Oh
to fall
headlong
into Mary's
sunken garden
and be tickled by
the tender exotics.

In
the shade
of the tunnel arbor
every leaf leans forward
to phantom light luring us toward
some distant promise, but were we there
looking back, would we but long for the phantom past?

In your blue depths are embedded the longing and love
of all who have stood here in starlight and wonder.

# Late-Summer Cricket

Long past frog time
a brown cricket
yellow with lily pollen
frenzied with mating lust
devours the quiet
alone—
I, sleepless at the window,
smell his dust.

Blue lichens climb a granite wall erasing cold certainty.

The mourning dove
in darkness
began his lonely song of love,
'Ohhow I love you.
Ohhow I love you.'
until he heard
through the chattering dawn,
'Onow I love you.
Onow I love you.'

*-for Pamela*

She remembered the white apple blossoms
he picked in moonlight.

## Ecliptic

Clop, clop, clop
the rhythmic clock
of horses' hooves
on courtyard stone
brings Anne to Henry
at Hampton in Richmond,
his astronomical clock
positioning the sun,
marking the months,
moons, tides on Thames,
the days without a son.
Click, click, click,
the nine months waiting,
the old world shaken
but to Henry only
more empty branches.
Clop, clop, clop,
Anne to a barge for the tide
to the Tower by the Thames,
the French sword waiting.
Elizabeth in her window
watches, sees Virgo
rising.

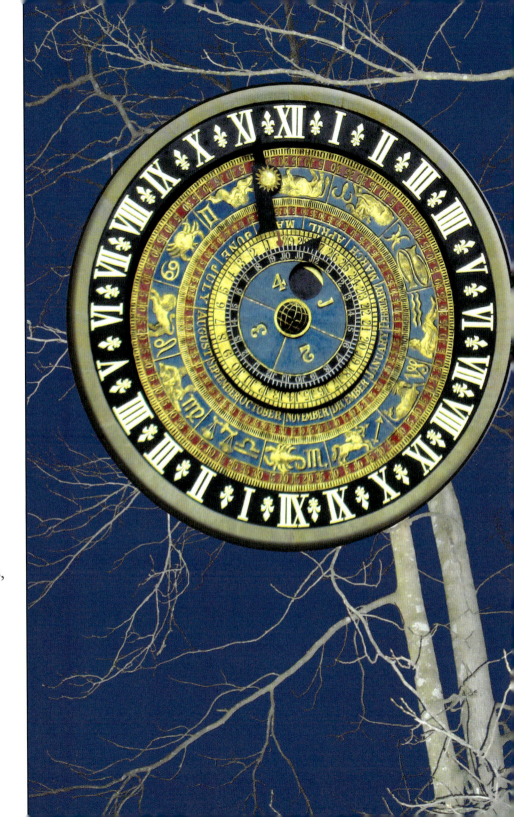

# Touchstone

Poems fall
as leaves
to streams.
Few float
for long.
One may
with time
imprint its
rare shape
in stone.

# Cruising April

He airbrushed their sly grins
into bolts of red laughter,
took their bluff to a violet edge.
They blazed on the pale beach,
in black spandex, waiting the swimmer
to crawl dripping from Chaos.
They had come to sin easily and well,
come to roll with fire dragons, track
white sand spots across dark negative souls.
Though I, the jarring black bird
in the frayed oak of winter,
had taught each Paradise was lost,
but obviously not completely.

The human heart inscrutable as God;
interpret either at your peril.

# Ephemerals

In silence
they break through forest floors
even before noisy, cyclic cicadas,
slipping through dead leaf cracks,
transforming into yellow trout lilies,
blood root and white wake-robin,
pink shooting stars beside trillium,
and they spread across open fields,
scattering blue anemones and
purple violets under milk weed,
seeding galaxies of bluets huddled
in clusters on the dark earth
warming and thirsty for spring-
all prelude to the leafy, dream
canopy of oak, maple, willow,
yellow poplar, red bud, beech
explosion.

Did he remember her
in spring when wisteria dripped
from trees in drops of lavender,
smothering the family home
with its secret letters her sister-
his wife-switched
that doomed them?
Did he smell still the lilac
of her neck as she traced violet
scars he carried from Argonne?
When did he know the secret
even his wife did not know
that would doom them?

There should have been children's children called
from evening play to shield the rising night.

In the death
of our fathers
we are made
more vulnerable.
Our only shelters are
love and memory.

Blind John Milton
saw Satan chained
on the Lake of Fire
dreaming of Eve
alone in the Garden.
We still wear
his epic chains.

Peel the sunset from the night sky
and stick it in our pocket.

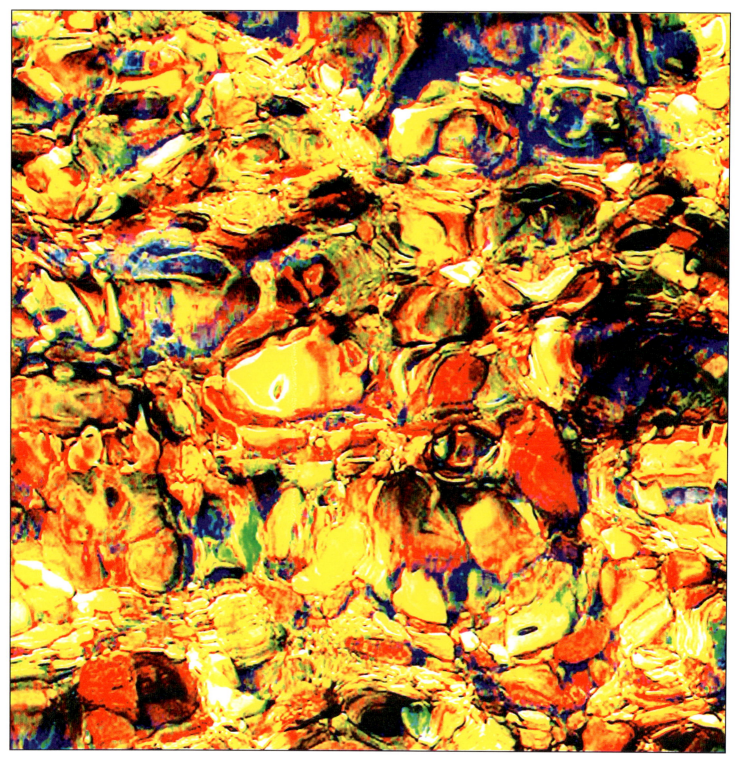

114

## Winter Crossing

In the sheen
of afternoon sun
spirits of Cherokee
cross New River
on their way home,
leaving the paths
of betrayal behind.

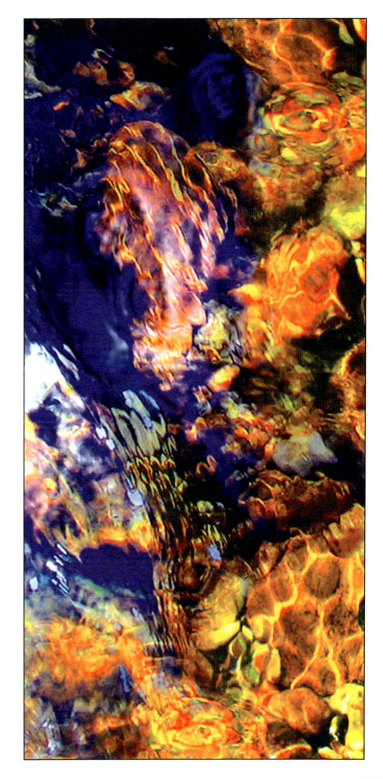

# Wind Break

I saw
the golden leaf let go
spiral through Indian wind
the break clean of cell and vein
long in winter others hang
twisted in their drying
to brown apparition
hardly leaf at all
no vein will break for you
in the windless cell you wait
the drip of sap to dead leaf
were I wind
I would know

## Pond Spirit

From the window she watches
fog rise from her father's pond,
cold ghosts caught at sunrise,
marking where summer dies
deep in the belly of a catfish
unaware as it filters bottom mud
that it is over above and
all has turned back from going.
Wind has matted the straw fields,
red sourwood trees are left
shattered by fleeing blackbirds,
death sinks degree by degree
until the catfish heart is ice
and old women who never loved
count the ghosts of October.

# Snake Handler at the Fair

"Watch carefully," she said,
"I'm new with rattlers."
Not a fool among us believed that.
She could have been of the Cult
for the way her delicate fingers
slipped through the cool diamond coils
and stroked him straight until
he yawned milk white venom
into a sterile, empty cup.
We burned from the easy way
she took his poison.

# Flowering Bloodroot

I should have taken you deep in woods
rammed against a scaling hickory
shinning you like a naked boy
up rough pine bark
or rolled you in needles digging
into black, slick leaf rot
all illusions peeled
lying wet among fire ants and slugs
no more pretense of love
back to grunt
your liberation complete
had you not taken me
so deep into the woods.

# The Persimmon Tree in October

Soft fruit drops like bits of autumn sun
with every notch the surveyor hacks
to mark the turn at the iron stake,
lines drawn, fragmentation complete—
only I hear Lear in the pine trees' roar.
You remember the day your father
marked this very corner by the pond, recall
the red bud tree she thought was peach—
always more bloom than fruit, yet love,
love strained at times to the edge of freedom,
but you never broke.
Those hard green summers have softened,
the bitter fruit ripe, near rotting.
I sit eating warm persimmons,
watch you watching the cornered land
all the way to where we began.

The woods
are burning
sumac, birch,
and beech-
all that will
not keep.

Through a window of ash
hills soften in autumn mist
and memory of summers
when we held life easily
between us, so careless
to time's passing, beyond
the reach of snow as if
the season of the green leaf
would last forever and ever.

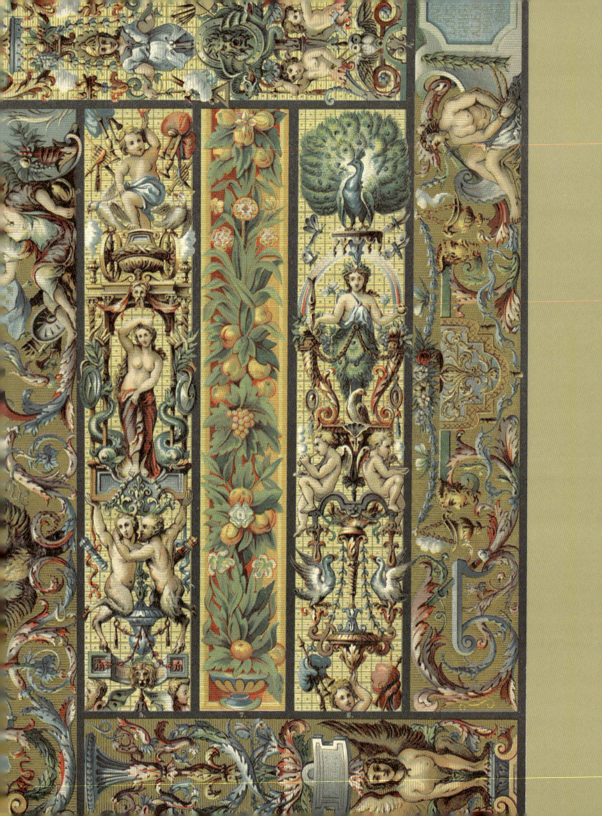

# Crazy Old Lilly

Crazy Old Lilly wipes holes in fog
to see Christmas in other windows
where peppermint breath shadows love.
Fox grape wine left uncorked
to sour for a man who, one sip taken,
rode away on a horse to Virginia Beach.
Crazy Old Lilly, fermented,
all stopped up,
bakes on the hearth,
crushing winter walnuts still
afraid of a horse and Virginia Beach.

*Noel! Noel! Hell to Noel!*
*Damn the dried up meat,*
*him, his horse, and Virginia Beach.*

Crazy Old Lilly, cool your fire,
rake for the roasted meat,
it's a hundred miles to Virginia Beach;
sip your warm fox grape wine
till it's nine hundred miles.
They'll never see you cry
through fogged up windows,
nodding, nodding,
to open fire….
Crazy Old Lilly
in walnut ash
carried on wind
for a hundred miles.

# Measuring Water Oaks

Sunday afternoon too hot for sitting
I wander to the bridge shade of Mill Road
to cool and lose myself in the creek trickle
and dream of a lost Saturday afternoon—
corn rows furrowed, the plow unhitched and
a Cox or Reeves, a Crouse or Collins
following the wagon path with grain
to Belk Mill and the water oak shade.
What bob-cat tales, coon hunting yarns rose
over the rumble of shaker, hopper, millstones
to settle in sweet corn dust on rafters?
Who kept count of grinding hours
of summer rain stored in the mill pond?
What longing, loneliness, what love
for these who gathered an afternoon
to swap six-foot views of the universe?
The mill pond dam is broken-
the wheel, the shaft, the shaker
washed away with gray boards, now
the only vibration, a stranger's truck
hurries to town, soon lost in silence.
My six-one shadow ripples in the creek,
longs to break and run with water—
the oaks brood, sucking the sun.

# Winter Solstice

Staring shyly into the dark eye of a black box camera,
she sits with her sisters on a stack of stove wood,
warmed by morning sun and hovering breath of young men
waiting for the end of school and spring's possibilities.
Late June came with ripening fields but vague promises,
then an assassin and a archduke met in distant Sarajevo.
When the world crawled from the trenches,
she was left empty with limited possibilities.
In despair she gave herself to Christ as sacrifice,
settling for a relationships of cold night certainty
measured by the stack of split wood and long distance
but specific promises.

# Tate

You would see him come
in a fog of starving dogs,
hear the flapping soles long before
dirty toes like terrapin heads
reached the screened back porch—
come to gut the hogs, salt the hams,
split the wood, cook the cane to molasses--
whatever would keep the winter, pay the store.
"How you stayin' warm these nights, Tate?"
"I just pulls me up another dog."
His laugh was soft and deep in snuff.
"This the Christmas your boy's comin'?"
"Gone be here sure on 'is motorcycle
'n take me to Georgia where's warm."
After forty years alone
he began to fade with the cabin
like an old gray mule waiting
by a broken fence in dry weeds.
Winters hardened. The dogs went off
one by one in the woods to stay.
All was vanishing, even the store.
We hardly knew he had gone until
the morning we carried him cake and candies—
three days dead on a worn road map
of the two Carolinas with half inch of Georgia.

# Count the rivers you have crossed

will cross, would cross if time were stone-
Indians Oconee, Cattachoochee, Catawba,
Kanawha, Rappahannock, Potomac, Savannah,
Shenandoah, Susquehanna- rivers of rainbow
Red, Yellow and Green- the Little, Leaf, Lost,
you did not know you crossed the Flint, Flat,
the Fox, the New, Deep, Devils, too- and those
sad rivers of Wind, Powder, Snake, and Platte,
a Mad, Big Two-Hearted, Mystic, Hackensack-
the wide rivers of Arkansas, Ohio, Columbia,
Missouri, Mississippi- and those still rising
in the east- Thames, Stour, Tiber, Seine, Arno,
Rhine, Danube, and Po- holy Jordan, Ganges,
ancient Nile- the Mekong and Yangtze far from
home, the Tokoro, Teshio you'll never cup with
dirty fingers or have one chance to wet a toe.

# Jennie Copeland

She collected her life in empty fruit jars hidden
on the back shelf among summer preserves,
jars of old pennies, quarters, a few silver dollars.
Each summer she promised herself a Greyhound tour
through the lattice shadows of New Orleans.
In time she learned to ignore the sprawling freshmen,
their naked tight jeans crotched near her hands
as she lavished on them one day each spring
the ecstasy of Sarah Teasdale they could never spell
and who preferred the music of unmuffled truck.

All passed her close as travelers on a bus.

Her life was there still waiting to be opened
by the nervous fingers of a younger man or shattered
and spilled over the ragged head of a piano player
drunk on smoldering jazz in the Vieux Carre—
all there still when they found her
in the bloated corner among sticky pennies
and broken preserves.

# The Garner House

Boards spring
the squirrels are in
a nail is loose
wind crawls under rusting tin
rotting rain comes with sour breath
and dirty teeth to chew the hall
eager weeds claw, claw, claw
the porch drops like a broken jaw
windows stare with blind holes—
Like a bleached, gutted turtle
the house sits
lost in bitter weeds
and brittle straw—
It took but a year
to take it with you.

Guide us through this place of spirit clouds lest we stray or stay.

# September

In
the high
meadows
late
summer
comes
through
straw
dragging
autumn
in its
teeth.

# Winter

With lead feet you sink
into our gray depths—
Oh what is left of you
in this noisy house
you swept too clean?
Now all is ours
and we are clutter.
Each year we gather still
though a stitched mouth cries,
'Remember me'
softer than the dust
we blow from
old Christmas bells.

This is the time of the gray heron
and the bare willow caught
in winter's light.

# The Mangum Sisters

Once a widow
I saw with her sisters
in a field of yellow straw
like black birds dipping
among the broom sedge
cut to clean the hearth,
sweep spiders from rooms
few ever knew—
dry, brittle women
with their trunks
always packed
and waiting.
I can hear still
the thump of empty trunks
pulled down broken steps,
see wind sweep the cold hearth,
and feel the spiders coming
through the frozen straw.

The scattered branches of a sycamore tree shake midnight snow
while the hawthorn scratches its name on the face of a frozen pond.
Neither remembers in the wait of December what curled buds know.

# Branches

We trained the fir tree
many summers to hold
holy light of mid-winter
as though we would keep
its hungry top tethered
for our sole delight.
We watched one evening
it reclaimed so easily
in a dark lesson of snow.
Too soon it grew
beyond our reach,
carrying the golden string
toward waiting springs
not meant for us to know,
adding branch to branches
filled with winged seed
for wind to plant in earth
and spill on distant seas.

A lone grackle drags morning across a pond of melting snow,
tipping earth toward hope and spring.

Made in the USA
San Bernardino, CA
09 October 2014